DO YOU REALLY WANT

TO VISIT A WETLAND?

WRITTEN BY BRIDGET HEOS · ILLUSTRATED BY DANIELE FABBRI

Amicus Illustrated is published by Amicus
P.O. Box 1329, Mankato, MN 56002
www.amicuspublishing.us

Library of Congress Cataloging-in-Publication Data
Heos, Bridget, author.
 Do you really want to visit a wetland? / by Bridget Heos ;
illustrated by Daniele Fabbri. — First edition.
    pages cm. — (Do you really want to visit...?)
 Audience: K-3.
 Summary: "A child goes on an adventure to the Florida
Everglades, discovering what the climate is like and
encountering many animals and plants that live in wetlands.
Includes world map of wetlands and glossary"— Provided
by publisher.
 Includes bibliographical references.
 ISBN 978-1-60753-454-9 (library binding) —
ISBN 978-1-60753-669-7 (ebook)
1. Wetland ecology—Juvenile literature. 2. Wetlands—
Juvenile literature. I. Fabbri, Daniele, 1978- ill. II. Title.
III. Series: Do you really want to visit—?
 QH541.5.M3H46 2015
 577.68—dc23   2013028469

Editor: Rebecca Glaser
Designer: Kathleen Petelinsek

Printed in the United States of America at
Corporate Graphics in North Mankato, Minnesota.
10 9 8 7 6 5 4 3 2

ABOUT THE AUTHOR

Bridget Heos is the author of more than 60 books for children, including many Amicus Illustrated titles and her recent picture book *Mustache Baby* (Houghton Mifflin Harcourt, 2013). She lives on the prairie of Kansas City with her husband and four children.

ABOUT THE ILLUSTRATOR

Daniele Fabbri was born in Ravenna, Italy, in 1978. He graduated from Istituto Europeo di Design in Milan, Italy, and started his career as a cartoon animator, storyboarder, and background designer for animated series. He has worked as a freelance illustrator since 2003, collaborating with international publishers and advertising agencies.

A visit to a wetland would help you ace your school report. Do you really want to go? It will be very . . . wet. But wetlands are also full of interesting animals, and only some of them will want to eat you.

Be prepared for water everywhere. You'll need hip waders. And don't bring a regular boat. You'll need an airboat with a big propeller above water so it doesn't get stuck in the muck.

Don't forget the bug spray and sunscreen. Ready? Now, you're off to explore the swamps, marshes, and sloughs of the Florida Everglades!

Start at the Shark River Slough. (Say: *sloo*) It looks like a big, still marsh, but the water moves through here like a slow river.

Don't worry. The bull sharks that the slough is named after live farther downstream. You might see rats or snakes. Uh-oh! Your boat is stuck.

Time to get out and push—and put on those waders. Don't touch the saw grass! It *is* as sharp as a saw. It rots and forms the muck you're stuck in.

Too bad you can't glide across the water like that
water moccasin, which is highly poisonous.

Lucky for you, the snake finds a frog for lunch. And finally, your boat breaks free. Now you can continue your tour.

People have drained half the Everglades to build houses and farms. Animals like the apple snail have lost some habitat. This affects the food chain. Birds, turtles, and alligators need the apple snail for food.

Luckily, rainfall still feeds much of the wetlands. Clouds are rolling in right now. The Everglades are surrounded on three sides by water. That creates 55 inches (140 cm) of rain per year. And when it rains, the water rises! Head west to the Big Cypress Swamp.

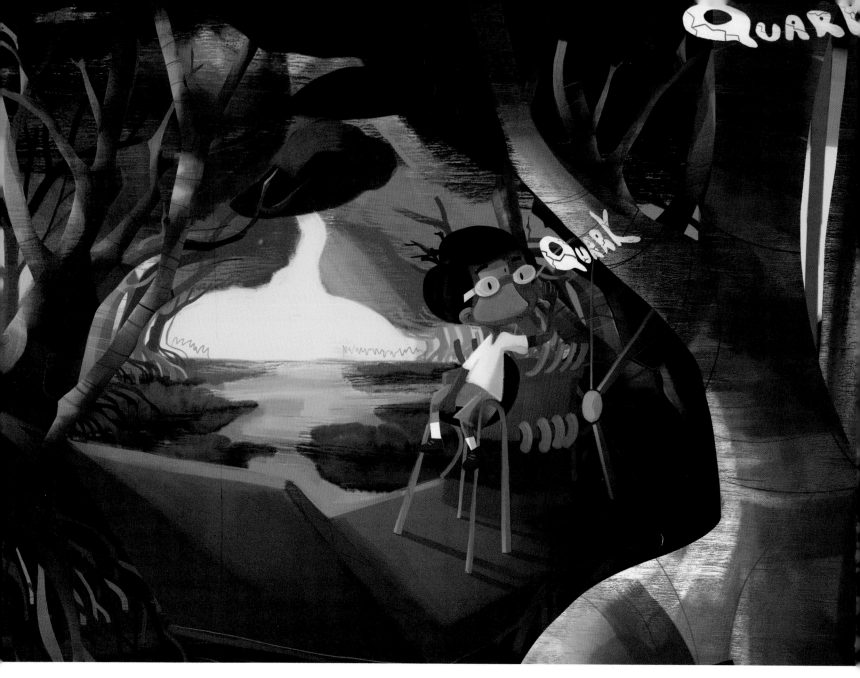

The trees overhead make it dark and
a little eerie. What's that sound?

"Quark, quark, quark." Oh, cute! It's a nest of alligators, and they're hatching. Somebody else thinks they're cute too.

Their mother! Alligators are good mamas.
That's bad for you. Quick, paddle away!

Head south toward the Gulf of Mexico. Here, the water mixes with the ocean and gets saltier.

This is a saltwater swamp. You can see the roots of the mangrove trees that grow here. And if you're lucky, you'll see an American crocodile. Crocodiles prefer salt water to freshwater. They are more rare than alligators, and very shy. The Everglades is the only place on earth where alligators and crocodiles coexist.

The Everglades is a fragile ecosystem. If we don't take care of it, we'll lose it. Nobody wants that, right manatee? Whoa, a manatee! A rare sight, indeed! Now you can go home and ace your report.

WETLANDS OF THE WORLD

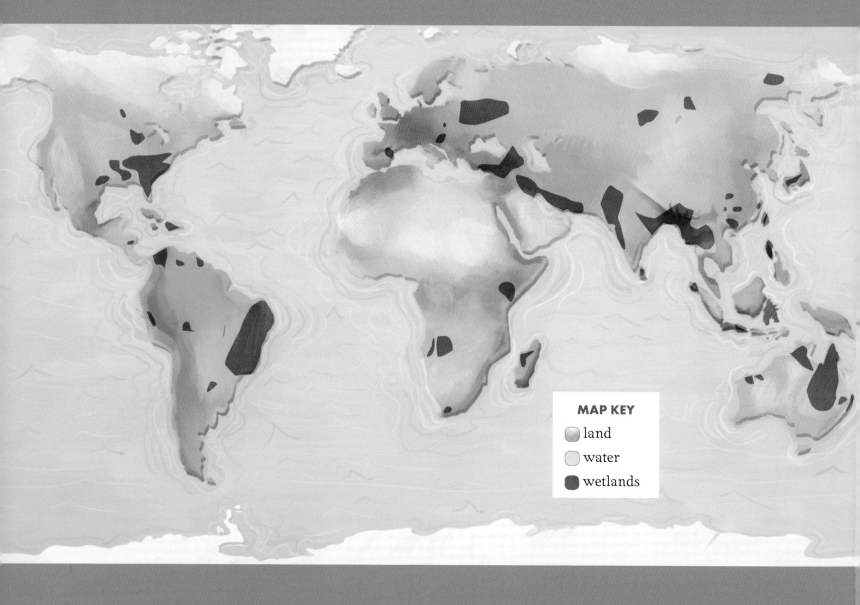

MAP KEY

- land
- water
- wetlands

SAVE THE WETLANDS

Wetlands such as the Everglades are drained to supply water to people living nearby. No matter where you live, freshwater is a limited resource and should not be wasted. To conserve water:

- Turn off the water when not in use.

- Take short showers.

- If your parents buy a new toilet, ask them to consider a low-flow toilet, which wastes less water when it flushes.

- Grow native plants, which only need rainwater.

GLOSSARY

ecosystem A community of animals and plants interacting with each other and their environment.

freshwater Water in rivers, lakes and wetlands that is not very salty.

marsh An area of low, wet land with tall grasses and reeds.

poisonous Harmful and likely to make a person sick or even die.

saw grass A marsh plant with sharp edges that could hurt you; also called sedge.

slough (*sloo*) A slow moving river. It is a type of marsh.

swamp An area of wet, spongy ground similar to a marsh, but with bigger plants and trees.

water moccasin A poisonous snake that hides in or near swamps and marshes in the southeastern United States; it is also called a cottonmouth.

wetland An area where there is a lot of moisture in the soil.

READ MORE

Bredeson, Carmen. **Baby Animals of the Wetlands**. Berkeley Heights, NJ: Enslow Elementary, 2011.

Katz Cooper, Sharon. **Marshes and Pools**. Chicago: Raintree, 2010.

Kaye, Cathryn Berger. **Make a Splash!: A Kid's Guide to Protecting Our Oceans, Lakes, Rivers, & Wetlands**. Minneapolis: Free Spirit Pub. Inc., 2013.

Newland, Sonya. **Wetland Animals**. Mankato, Minn.: Smart Apple Media, 2012.

WEBSITES

Conservation in Action: Everglades
http://video.nationalgeographic.com/video/environment/going-green-environment/conservation-in-action/everglades/
Watch this video to learn how people are working to save the Florida Everglades.

Florida Dept. of Environmental Protections
http://www.dep.state.fl.us/secretary/kids/postcards/everglades.htm
View facts, pictures, and quizzes on the Florida Everglades.

Freshwater Wetlands
http://kids.nceas.ucsb.edu/biomes/freshwaterwetlands.html
Visit this website to read about wetland plants, animals, and climate.

Ponds and Wetlands Science
http://www.earthskids.com/ek_science-pond-wetland.htm
Learn how wetlands are beneficial and vital to the environment.

Every effort has been made to ensure that these websites are appropriate for children. However, because of the nature of the Internet, it is impossible to guarantee that these sites will remain active indefinitely or that their contents will not be altered.